Move on with Decimals

By Br... ...lin Bass

Curriculum Visions

There's much more online including videos

You will find multimedia resources covering a wide range of topics at:

www.CurriculumVisions.com

CurriculumVisions is a subscription web site.

A CVP Book
Copyright © 2009 Atlantic Europe Publishing

Series Concept
Brian Knapp, BSc, PhD

Text contributed by
Brian Knapp, BSc, PhD, and Colin Bass, BSc, MA

Editors
Lorna Gilbert, Barbara Carragher, and Gillian Gatehouse

Senior Designer
Adele Humphries, BA, PGCE

Illustrations
David Woodroffe

Designed and produced by
Atlantic Europe Publishing

Printed in China by
WKT Company Ltd

Curriculum Visions Move on with Maths – Decimals
A CIP record for this book is available from the British Library

ISBN: 978 1 86214 559 7

Picture credits
All photographs are from the Earthscape Picture Library and ShutterStock collections.

This product is manufactured from sustainable managed forests. For every tree cut down at least one more is planted.

Look out for these sections to help you learn more about each topic:

Remember... This provides a summary of the key concept(s) on each two-page entry. Use it to revise what you have learned.

Can you do this? These problems reinforce the concepts learned on a particular spread, and can be used to test existing knowledge.

Answers to the problems set in the 'Move on with Maths' series can be found at: **www.curriculumvisions.com/moveOnAnswers**

Place value

To make it easy for you to see exactly what we are doing, you will find coloured columns behind the numbers in all the examples on this and the following pages. This is what the colours mean:

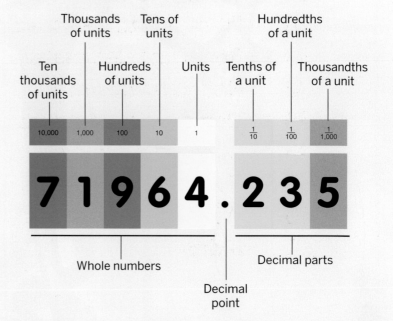

Ten thousands of units — 10,000
Thousands of units — 1,000
Hundreds of units — 100
Tens of units — 10
Units — 1
Tenths of a unit — $\frac{1}{10}$
Hundredths of a unit — $\frac{1}{100}$
Thousandths of a unit — $\frac{1}{1,000}$

7 1 9 6 4 . 2 3 5

Whole numbers

Decimal parts

Decimal point

Contents

Using a decimal point

Numbers with decimal parts must be written down very carefully.

Decimals are made of whole numbers and parts of numbers separated by a decimal point. To help you to see how decimals work, we have used coloured columns to make it easier to see the value of each number.

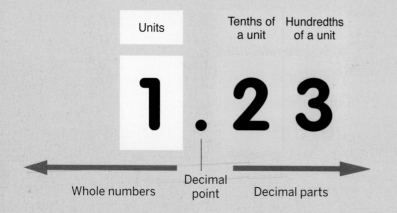

The number **1.23** is one whole unit, two tenths of a unit, and three hundredths of a unit.
It is said as "One point two three".

1.23

Here is how **325.23** is made up.

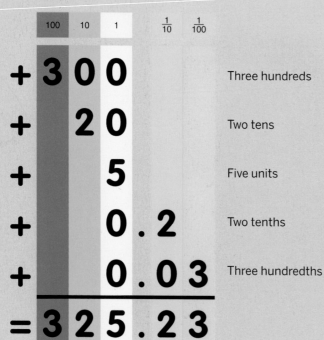

It is made of hundreds, tens, and units, and then (to the right of the decimal point) tenths and hundredths of units.

This is the number without the coloured columns. It is three hundred and twenty five point two three.

325.23

Mick had arrived on holiday in the USA. He wanted to send a postcard home. He found one priced **$1.23** on a street stall. He had not yet got used to US currency but he did know that **1.23** was bigger than **1** and less than **2**, so he handed the vendor **$2** and held out his hand for the change.

Jacob received a letter from his savings bank saying that they had added interest to his account, so he now had **£325.23** saved. He knew that **£3.25** would be enough to buy **4** slim-fast milk shakes. So, moving the decimal point one place to the right, **£32.50** would buy **40** milk shakes. And, moving the decimal point one place to the right again, **£325.00** would buy **400** of them. Jacob felt quite rich!

 Remember... The decimal point tells us which are whole units and which are parts of units.

Can you do this? On a sheet of paper, write one and seven tenths as a decimal.

Decimals as shapes

One way to understand decimals is to write out the problem in shapes.

You can use shapes to show a number that has a decimal point. A unit is made up of ten tenths or a hundred hundredths. Here's how it is used to show **2.45**:

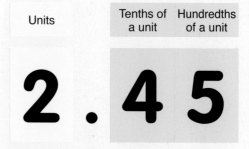

Units	Tenths of a unit	Hundredths of a unit

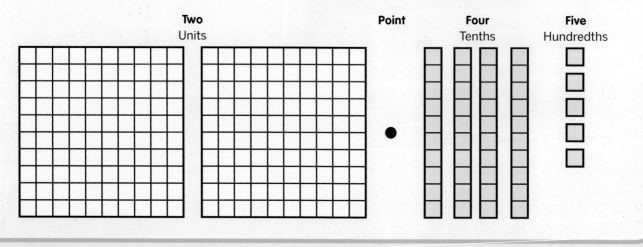

Two
Units

Point

Four
Tenths

Five
Hundredths

LOW
BRIDGE

13'-6"

Simon is driving a van he has rented. He was warned that it is **2.45 metres** high. When he comes to a low bridge marked "clearance **13 ft 6 inches**", he stops to think before trying to drive under.

He knows that a metre is just over **3 feet**. He also knows that **0.45** is just less than ½, which is **0.5**.

He reckons that **2 metres** will be a little over **6 feet**. (It is about **6½ feet** actually.)

He does not need to struggle working out **2.45 metres**, because **3 metres** is more, and **3 metres** works out to a bit more than **9 feet** (9½ ft).

A **3 metre** van would easily go under the bridge, so his **2.45 metre** van will be fine.

He could have seen that clearly if he had got out of the van and looked at it and the bridge.

Actually, **2.45 metres** is almost exactly **8 feet**.

Oddly enough, Simon's rented van weighs **2.45 tonnes**. Simon comes to another rusty road sign:

"Weak bridge – maximum weight 3 tons."

Luckily, Simon remembers that a ton means an old British ton, which is almost exactly the same as a metric tonne. Actually, **1 ton = 1.017 tonnes**.

The letters "m g w" in the road sign mean "maximum gross weight". Maximum means the greatest allowed. Gross means that you have to include the weight of Simon and anything he has put into the van.

Simon weighs **80 kg**, which is **0.08 tonnes**. He guesses that his stuff weighs about twice as much as he does (that is, about **0.16 tonnes**).

So Simon and his goods weigh:

**2.45 + 0.08 + 0.16 tonnes
= 2.45 + 0.24 = 2.69 tonnes**

As **2.69** is less than **3**, it is safe to drive over the bridge.

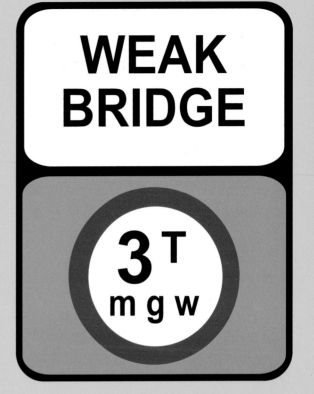

WEAK BRIDGE

3 T
m g w

Can you do this? A US gallon is about **3.79 litres**. An Imperial (British) gallon is about **4.55 litres**. Which kind of gallon of petrol would Simon's van go further on?

>>>>> **Remember...** Whatever size your number, the neighbouring numbers are always ten times smaller on the right, and they are less than one if they are to the right of the decimal point.

Decimals in money

It is easiest to use a money system in which numbers are multiples of ten.

Pounds and pence

Almost every currency in the world uses the decimal system to count in tens. The names for whole units and parts of a unit may be different, but they are all decimal currencies.

How we write a decimal currency depends on the unit we are using. For example, if we are using pounds, **59 pence** is written down as **£0.59**, because **59 pence** is less than a pound. But if we are using pence, then **59 pence** is expressed in whole numbers because the unit is the pence.

The same is true for other currencies, as you can see.

Pounds and pence

The pound is the unit of currency of the United Kingdom. A pound is made up of **100 pence**. The pound is a decimal currency because there are pence, tens of pence and hundreds of pence.

Tens of pence, but tenths of a pound

Units of pence, but hundredths of a pound

5 9
Pence (p)

0 . 5 9
Pounds (£)

59 pence is five 10 pence coins and nine 1 pence coins.

Euros and cents

The euro is the currency used in 15 of the 27 countries of the European Union, with most others intending to use it as soon as they can. It is a decimal currency because each euro is divided into **100 cents**. One and two cent coins are made, but rarely used.

Tens of cents, but tenths of a euro

Units of cents, but hundredths of a euro

9 7
Cent (c)

0 . 9 7
Euro (€)

Euros and cents

>>> **Remember...** The world works in decimal currencies, meaning that they are organised in multiples of ten.

Dollars and cents

The dollar is the most widely used unit in the world. There are also coins with a value of part of a dollar, for example **10 cents** and **1 cent**. There are **100 cents** in a dollar.

The dollar is a decimal currency because cents, tens of cents and dollars (hundreds of cents) are all multiples of ten.

Tens of cents, but tenths of a dollar

Units of cents, but hundredths of a dollar

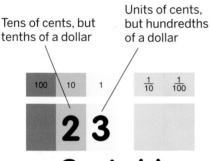

Cents (¢)

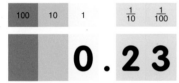

Dollars ($)

23 cents is two 10 cent coins and three 1 cent coins.

Dollars and cents

Rupees and paisa

The rupee is the unit of currency of India. A rupee consists of **100 paisa**. Because there are paisa, tens of paisa and rupees (hundreds of paisa), the rupee is also a decimal currency.

Tens of paisa, but tenths of a rupee.

Units of paisa, but hundredths of a rupee.

Paisa

Rupees (Rs)

47 paisa is four 10 paisa coins and seven 1 paisa coins.

Pesos and centavos

The currency used in many South and Central American countries, and some other Spanish speaking countries elsewhere, is the peso, from an old Spanish word meaning "weight". It has different values in different countries, and they change all the time. The peso also is a decimal currency. A peso is divided into **100 centavos**.

Tens of centavos, but tenths of a peso.

Units of centavos, but hundredths of a peso.

Centavos (c)

Pesos ($)

Decimals in science

All scientists in the world use a decimal system called the metric system. The rule is: in science use metric.

The height of a liquid in a flask was measured using a scale in millimetres. It was exactly **234 mm** high.

In this case, all of the numbers would be to the left of the decimal point and so the decimal point is not used at all.

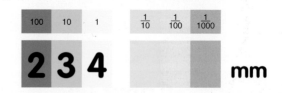

We can record the height in centimetres (centimetres are ten times as big as millimetres).

To change our measurement from millimetres to centimetres, we divide by **10**:

234 ÷ 10 = 23.4 cm

Notice that when we divide by **10**, we move the numbers one place to the right.

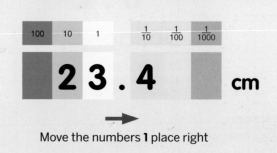

Move the numbers **1** place right

We can record the height in metres (metres are **100** times as big as centimetres).

To change from centimetres to metres, divide by **100**:

23.4 ÷ 100 = 0.234 m

Notice that when we divide by **100**, we move the numbers two places to the right.

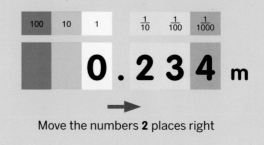

Move the numbers **2** places right

In this case, we read in metres first, then change to centimetres, and finally millimetres.

The height of the liquid in this flask has been read as **0.379 m**.

| 100 | 10 | 1 | $\frac{1}{10}$ | $\frac{1}{100}$ | $\frac{1}{1000}$ |

0.379 m

There are **100 cm** in a metre. If we wanted to express the number as centimetres, we would multiply it by **100**:

0.379 × 100 = 37.9 cm

Notice that when we multiply by **100**, we move the numbers two places to the left.

37.9 cm

Move the numbers **2** places left

We could also express the height in millimetres. There are **10** millimetres in a centimetre. To change to millimetres, we multiply by **10**, moving the numbers one place to the left:

37.9 × 10 = 379 mm

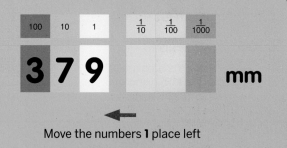

379 mm

Move the numbers **1** place left

 Remember… To divide a number by **10**, move the numbers one place to the right. This is the same as moving the decimal point one place to the left.

To multiply a number by **10**, move the numbers one place to the left. This is the same as moving the decimal point one place to the right.

Can you do these in your head?

What is **1.75 metres** in centimetres? What is **3,950 millimetres** in metres?

Adding with decimals

Line up each number at the decimal point.
Then adding with decimals is the same as
adding whole numbers.

For example,

345.23 + 467.39 = ?

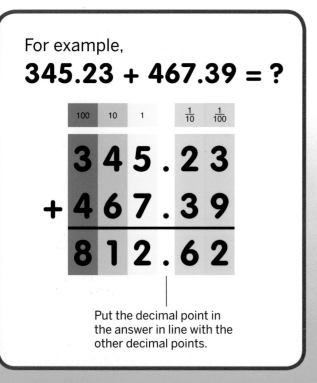

100	10	1	$\frac{1}{10}$	$\frac{1}{100}$
3	**4**	**5 .**	**2**	**3**
+4	**6**	**7 .**	**3**	**9**
8	**1**	**2 .**	**6**	**2**

Put the decimal point in
the answer in line with the
other decimal points.

Decimal stretch

Jilly was working on a science project.
She had discovered that a rubber band
stretched **0.56 cm** when she hung a
100 g weight from it, and **1.96 cm** when
she hung a **350 g** weight from it.

Jilly then needed to add together
the two measurements she had made
to find out how far the rubber band
would stretch if she hung a **450 g** weight
from it. For this she needed to add two
decimal numbers as you can see here.

The answer was **2.52**.

A zero (**0**) is written here to
make it absolutely clear that
the number is less than **1**.

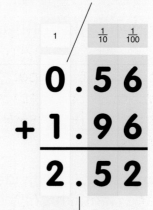

1	$\frac{1}{10}$	$\frac{1}{100}$
0 .	**5**	**6**
+1 .	**9**	**6**
2 .	**5**	**2**

The numbers are lined up
and then added together in
the normal way.

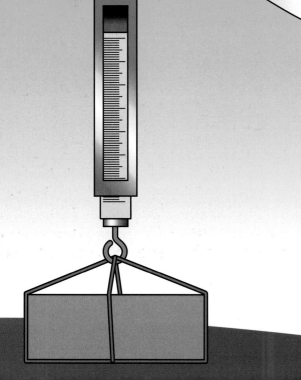

Making decimals whole numbers while you add

If you are still unsure about adding decimal numbers, you can turn them into whole numbers by making the decimal parts the same length, then dropping the decimal point. Add the whole numbers together and then put the decimal point back into the answer.

But beware: if the numbers have units, make sure the units are the same before your start (see pages 10–11).

James wanted to measure the length of two pieces of wire to be used in a science experiment. The first piece measured **3.56 m** and the second length measured **4.76 m**. Notice the decimal point is two numbers from the right in each case.

1 As he did not feel sure about decimals yet, he decided to turn his decimals into whole numbers while he added.

2 He lined up both numbers so the decimal points were above one another. Then he removed the decimal point.

In this way **3.56** became **356** and **4.76** became **476**. He added **356 + 476** together. The total was **832**.

3 Finally, he had to convert his number back to a decimal number, so he placed the decimal point two numbers from the right in his answer, so that **832** became **8.32 m**.

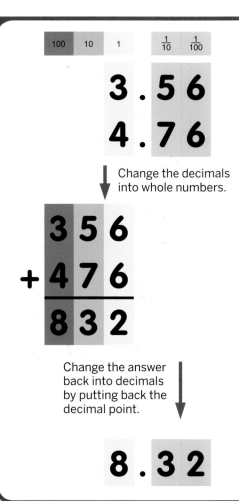

Change the decimals into whole numbers.

Change the answer back into decimals by putting back the decimal point.

Can you do these?
0.375 + 1.125 = ?
4.47 + 9.78 = ?

Work the answers out on a separate piece of paper.

 Remember... To add with decimals, either add normally, making sure you line up the numbers around the decimal point, or convert to whole numbers, add them together, and then convert back.

Different decimal lengths

You make up unequal decimal numbers with 0s.

1 If you find that you have to add numbers of a different decimal length line them up around the decimal point.

Line up the two numbers using the decimal point.

100	10	1	$\frac{1}{10}$	$\frac{1}{100}$

2 7 6 . 3 5
   5 6 . 1

2 Then put a **0** at the right hand end in the decimal spaces as shown here:

2 7 6 . 3 5
   5 6 . 1 0

Fill in a **0** here.

3 Then add as usual.

   2 7 6 . 3 5
+   5 6 . 1 0
   3 3 2 . 4 5

A whole number is really a decimal number where everything to the right of the decimal is **0**.

3 5 7
3 9 . 3 7

Then add.

Place a decimal point here.

Fill in a **0** here for every decimal place of the other number.

   3 5 7 . 0 0
+   3 9 . 3 7
   3 9 6 . 3 7

Children from Charles's class measured rainfall figures for a week. Because they forgot to agree beforehand, they did it differently. These were the results. What was the rainfall for the week?

Sunday	0.1 cm
Monday	1.5 mm
Tuesday	2.30 cm
Wednesday	5 cm
Thursday	11 mm
Friday	0
Saturday	.2 mm

First we must decide whether we want the answer in mm or cm and change all the measurements to what we choose. Charles chose cm. Check these conversions have been done correctly (See pages 10 and 11).

Sunday	0.1 cm
Monday	0.15 cm
Tuesday	2.30 cm
Wednesday	5 cm
Thursday	1.1 cm
Friday	0
Saturday	0.02 cm

Now we line up the decimal points, fill up blank decimal places with **0's**, and add the numbers up.

The rainfall for the whole week was **8.67 cm**, assuming all the readings were accurate.

```
  0.10
  0.15
  2.30
  5.00
  1.10
  0.00
  0.02
 ------
  8.67
```

Can you do this? Convert all the rainfall figures to millimetres before adding them up.

Give your working out on a separate piece of paper, then compare your answer to the sum above.

 Remember… To add whole numbers and decimals, turn the whole number into a decimal by adding a decimal point and as many **0's** as necessary.

Subtract decimals with the exchanging method

To subtract two numbers, simply line them up around the decimal point and begin your subtraction.

34.23 − 26.39 = ?

Both numbers line up around the decimal point.

10	1	$\frac{1}{10}$	$\frac{1}{100}$
3	4 .	2	3
2	6 .	3	9

1 Subtract from the right (the hundredths column). Take the lower number from the upper. Because **3 − 9** won't go, exchange one from the tenths column on the left and balance this out by adding **1** to the lower number of the tenths column as shown.
   Now the subtraction is **13 − 9 = 4**. Write down **4** in the hundredths column.

$$3\ 4\ .\ 2\ 3$$
$$-\ 2\ 6\ .\ 3\ 9$$
$$4$$

Exchange **1** from the tenths column, making a total of **13** hundredths.

Balance this out by adding **1** to the bottom of the left column.

2 Now subtract from the tenths column, then the units and finally the tens. So you have now subtracted from right to left.
   The exchanging numbers are shown here. Check them out.

$$3\ 4\ .\ 2\ 3$$
$$-\ 2\ 6\ .\ 3\ 9$$
$$7\ .\ 8\ 4$$

Can you do this?
57.14 − 39.25 = ?

Work the answer out on a separate piece of paper.

16

Sophie bought a blouse for **£26.99** and made lots of smaller purchases in the same shop. The total bill was **£58.17**. At home she found there was a button missing from the blouse. She took it back to the shop. They could not replace it, so they gave her the money back. How much had she spent in the shop in the end?

1 Put the money Sophie paid for the blouse (**£26.99**) below the total bill (**£58.17**), lining up the decimal points.

Subtract from the right (the hundredths column). Take the lower number from the upper. Because **7 – 9** won't go, exchange one from the tenths column on the left and balance this out by adding **1** to the lower number of the tenths column as shown.

Now the subtraction is **17 – 9 = 8**. Write down **8** in the hundredths column.

Exchange **1** from the tenths column, making a total of **17** hundredths.

Balance this out by adding **1** to the bottom of the left column.

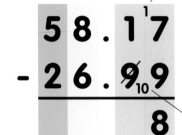

2 Now subtract from the tenths column, then the units and finally the tens. So you have now subtracted from right to left.

The exchanging numbers are shown here. Check them out.

$$
\begin{array}{r}
5\,8\,.\,\overset{1}{1}\,\overset{1}{7} \\
-\;2\,\overset{}{6}_{7}\,.\,\overset{}{9}\,\overset{}{9}_{10} \\
\hline
3\,1\,.\,1\,8
\end{array}
$$

3 In the end, Sophie had spent **£31.18** in the shop.

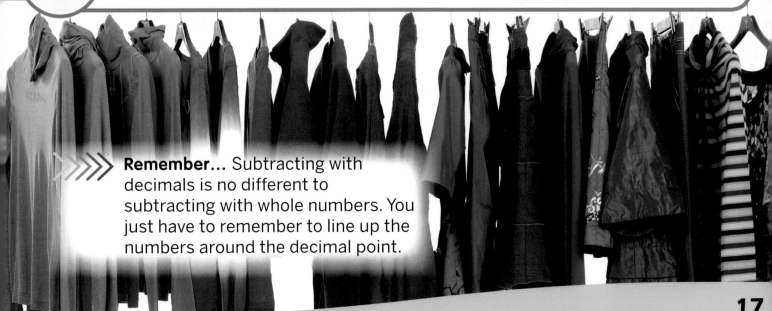

>>> **Remember...** Subtracting with decimals is no different to subtracting with whole numbers. You just have to remember to line up the numbers around the decimal point.

Subtract decimals by regrouping

Subtracting decimals can also be done by regrouping.

1 Line up the two numbers using the decimal point. In this case we are subtracting **1.72** from **2.5**.

Both numbers line up around the decimal point.

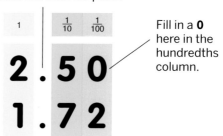

| 1 | $\frac{1}{10}$ | $\frac{1}{100}$ |

$$2 . 5\ 0$$
$$1 . 7\ 2$$

Fill in a **0** here in the hundredths column.

2 Start your subtraction on the right (the hundredths column). Take the lower number from the upper. Because **0 – 2** won't go, regroup one tenth as ten hundredths, reducing the tenths from **5** to **4** and increasing the hundredths by **10**.

  Now the subtraction is **10 – 2** = **8**. Write down **8**.

Regroup **1 tenth** from the top of the left column after the decimal point and make it **10 hundredths** at the top of the next column. This leaves **4 tenths** in the left column. Cross out the **5** and write a **4**.

$$2 . \overset{4}{\cancel{5}}\ \overset{1}{0}$$
$$-\ 1 . 7\ 2$$
$$\overline{8}$$

3 Move left to the other columns to complete your subtraction.

$$\overset{1}{\cancel{2}} . \overset{14}{\cancel{5}}\ \overset{1}{0}$$
$$-\ 1 . 7\ 2$$
$$\overline{0 . 7\ 8}$$

Can you do this?
7.5 – 3.94 = ?

Work the answer out on a separate piece of paper.

Emma's French horn needs a new mouthpiece. It must be a very accurate fit. The end of the mouthpiece is **24.20 mm** across and it needs a hole **12.82 mm** across bored in it. How thick will the walls of the mouthpiece be afterwards?

1 First we have to subtract **24.20 – 12.82**

10	1	$\frac{1}{10}$	$\frac{1}{100}$
2 4	.	2	0
– 1 2	.	8	2

2 Do this using the regrouping method as shown:

$$2\overset{3}{\cancel{4}}.\overset{11}{\cancel{2}}\overset{1}{0}$$
$$-\ 1\ 2\ .\ 8\ 2$$
$$\overline{1\ 1\ .\ 3\ 8}$$

3 Now remember that that is the thickness on both sides of the mouthpiece.

The thickness of the mouthpiece wall is **11.38 ÷ 2 = 5.69 mm**

$$2)\overline{1\ 1\ .\ 3\ \overset{1}{}8\overset{1}{}}$$
$$5\ .\ 6\ 9$$

Remember… You can subtract by regrouping or by exchanging as shown on page 16.

Multiplying a decimal

If you have to multiply a decimal by a whole number, you can use this simple technique.

6.5 × 7 = ?

1 Count and remember how many places of decimals you have. In this case it is **1** place.

2 Then convert the decimal number to a whole number. (**6.5** becomes **65**)
This is like changing **6.5 cm** into mm to do the multiplication. Later we change the answer back to cm.

The decimal number **6.5** has been moved one place to the left to make the whole number **65**.

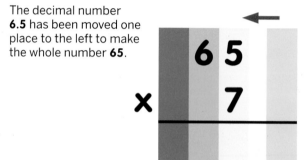

3 Multiply as you would for two whole numbers. That is: **7 × 65 = 455**.

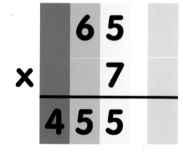

4 Now change the answer from a whole number back into a decimal number by putting the decimal point back from the right-hand end the same number of places as in the original decimal number.
In this case the number goes **1** place to the right. Notice the difference this makes to the value of the answer. It divides it by **10** from **455** to **45.5**.

Move the whole number **455** one place to the right and insert the decimal point to turn it back to the decimal number **45.5**.

Why does it work?

You really multiplied the decimal number by **10** when you moved the number one place to the left. Then, at the end, you divided the answer by **10** to reverse this change.

Titanium panels

NASA engineers were designing a part for the Space Shuttle. For this they needed a titanium panel **7 metres × 6.15 metres**. They needed to apply a very expensive special coating to the titanium panel. In order to find out the exact quantity of coating needed the engineers would first have to work out the area of their panel.

Area is worked out by multiplying length x width, so they needed to work out **7 x 6.15 metres**.

To simplify the sum, they needed to convert the decimal number in to a whole number. They needed to move the decimal point in **6.15** two places to the left to produce a whole number (**615**).

The multiplication would become **7 × 615 = 4,305**.

They then had to remember to put the decimal point two places back from the right-hand end. That makes it **43.05**. This is because **6.15** was multiplied by **100** when the number was moved, and **4,305** was divided by **100** when the number was moved back.

So the area of the titanium panel is **43.05 square metres**. The engineers could now order the right quantity of coating for the panel.

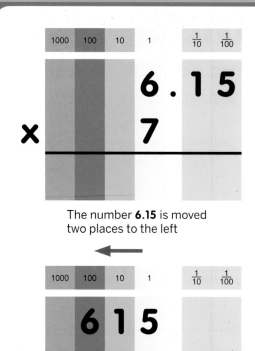

| 1000 | 100 | 10 | 1 | $\frac{1}{10}$ | $\frac{1}{100}$ |

$$6.15$$
$$\times \quad 7$$

The number **6.15** is moved two places to the left

| 1000 | 100 | 10 | 1 | $\frac{1}{10}$ | $\frac{1}{100}$ |

$$615$$
$$\times \quad 7$$
$$4305$$

$$43.05$$

The number is moved two places to the right.

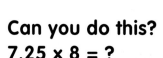

Can you do this?
7.25 x 8 = ?

Work the answer out on a separate piece of paper.

Remember...
To replace the decimal point correctly when multiplying.

Multiplying with decimals

Two decimal numbers can be multiplied together by first turning both of them into whole numbers.

Measuring the weed killer

Sean and Kelly's Dad wanted to buy some weed killer for the lawn on his way home from work. Unfortunately, he had forgotten to measure the lawn. He telephoned to ask the children to measure it for him. The lawn was a rectangle. Dad asked the children to measure the length and the width of the lawn in metres, and then multiply the two figures together to find out the total area of the lawn.

1

Sean measured the lawn very carefully. It was **6.15 m** wide and **7.1 m** long.

$$6.15 \times 7.1 = ?$$

There is an easier rule when both numbers to be multiplied are decimals. Make both numbers into whole numbers. Count and remember how many places you moved the decimal points altogether.

In this case the decimal point is moved one place to the right to change the decimal number **7.1** into the whole number **71**.

$$7.1 \Rightarrow 71$$

For the decimal number **6.15** the decimal point is moved two places to the right to produce the whole number **615**.

$$6.15 \Rightarrow 615$$

The moves for these two decimal numbers add up to a total of **3** decimal places.

Remember... You put the decimal point in the answer as many places from the right as the total decimal places in the numbers you multiplied.

2

Now multiply the whole numbers together in the normal way.

```
      6 1 5
  ×     7 1
─────────────
      6 1 5
  4 3 0 5 0
─────────────
  4 3 6 6 5
```

3

Place a decimal point in the answer **3** decimal places back from the right-hand end. In this way Sean and Kelly find out that the lawn area measures **43.665 m²**.

43.665

Sean and Kelly's Dad was very pleased when they told him their answer. When he arrived at the shop, he discovered that the weed killer was sold in packs containing enough to treat either **30** square metres, or **50** square metres. Dad could therefore confidently buy the 50-square-metre pack because he now knew that the 30-square-metre pack would be too small.

30 < 44 < 50

< means "is smaller than". Also, see page 38, where > means "is bigger than".

Can you do this?
2.25 x 1.23 = ?

Work the answer out on a separate piece of paper.

Checking the decimal point

It pays to find your own mistakes before anyone else does!
Here is a quick method of checking your decimals.

52.34 × 14 = ?

1 Write down the numbers you want to multiply together using only the number furthest to the left. Write **0's** in place of the others, and you have a simpler number to work with.

**52.34 is roughly 50
14 is roughly 10**

2 Multiply these two simpler numbers in your head, taking care about the total number of **0's** in your answer.

This should give you the approximate size of answer to the multiplication you are checking.

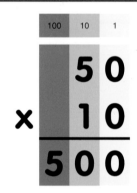

This is the rough answer worked out using long multiplication.

3 When we multiply **5,234 × 14** properly using long multiplication, the answer is exactly **73,276**. When we replace the decimal point, this becomes **732.76**.

But you can see that the rough check at least made sure that we knew the answer was in the hundreds rather than in the tens, thousands, and so on. This check took only a few seconds.

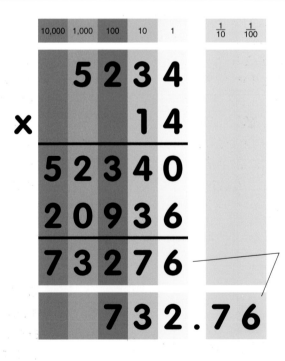

This is the exact answer worked out using long multiplication of the whole numbers and then replacing the decimal point as shown on pages 22–23.

Another example, using huge numbers also uses 'rounding'. For the calculation **5,678 × 87.65**:

5,678 × 87.65 = ?

1

Round up **5,678** to **6,000** and **87.65** to **90**.
    Now the problem is **6,000 × 90**.

5,678 is roughly 6,000
87.65 is roughly 90

6,000 × 90

2

Split up the long numbers to make them shorter and therefore easier to multiply.
    You can now multiply the simple numbers in your head in any order you wish to make the approximate answer **540,000**.

6,000 × 90
= 6 × 9 × 1,000 × 10
= 54 × 10,000
= 540,000

The correct answer is **497,676.70**, and as you can see, **540,000** is near enough to make us sure that we are getting the decimal point in the right place.

Brad bought two shirts costing **£37.99** each. He used his calculator to work out how much he would have to pay! The answer he got was **£7,598**. Not even Brad would be foolish enough to pay so much for two shirts. The answer should be about **£80** because **£37.99** is about **£40** and **£40 × 2 = £80**. Shift the decimal point two places to the left to see that Brad probably did not press the decimal point button hard enough when he typed **37.99**. He typed **3799** by mistake.

£7,598

£75.98

Remember... Rough working out only takes a few seconds, and these few seconds are well spent if we can be sure that the decimal point is in the right place.

Can you do this in your head?
Roughly, what is **2.7 × 3.142**?

Write your answer on a separate piece of paper.

Duviding by a whole number

Decimal points can be 'self-adjusting'.
Here is how.

When dividing a whole number into a decimal, just keep the decimal points lined up, and the decimal point in the answer will automatically be in the correct position.
   You can use either short or long division.

Pizza sharing

José bought a pizza for **£5.60** for himself and four friends. They divided it equally among the five of them and ate it. At the end of the meal the four friends wanted to pay José what they owed him.
   The calculation was:

5.60 ÷ 5 = ?

They did this by short division as follows:

---

1 Divide **5** into the first digit. The answer is **1**, remainder **0**. Put in a decimal point.

$$\begin{array}{r} 1\quad \tfrac{1}{10}\quad \tfrac{1}{100} \\ 5\overline{)\,5\,.\,6\,0} \\ 1\,.\,?\,? \end{array}$$

---

2 Divide **5** into the second digit, **6**. The answer is **1**, remainder **1**. Carry the remainder right to make **10**.

$$\begin{array}{r} 5\overline{)\,5\,.\,6\,{}^{1}0} \\ 1\,.\,1\,? \end{array}$$

---

3 Divide **5** into the third number, **10**. The answer is **2**, remainder **0**.

So each friend had to pay José **£1.12**.

$$\begin{array}{r} 5\overline{)\,5\,.\,6\,{}^{1}0} \\ 1\,.\,1\,2 \end{array}$$

Ben works it out

Ben wanted to compare accurately the thickness of a DVD box and a CD box so he would know how many DVDs he could get on the shelf where he used to keep his CDs. He stacked a sample of **15** DVD boxes along a table and measured the total length very carefully. It was **21.4 cm**. It was now easy for Ben to work out accurately how thick one of the DVD boxes would be.

1 Divide **15** into the first two digits. The answer is **1** with a remainder of **6**. Put in a decimal point. Bring down the next number, making **64**.

2 Divide **15** into the remainder (**64**). The answer is **4** with a remainder of **4**. Bring down the next digit, **0** to make **40**.

3 Divide **15** into the remainder, **40**. The answer is **2**, with remainder of **10**.

4 Divide **15** into the remainder, and so on to get as many decimal places as you need.

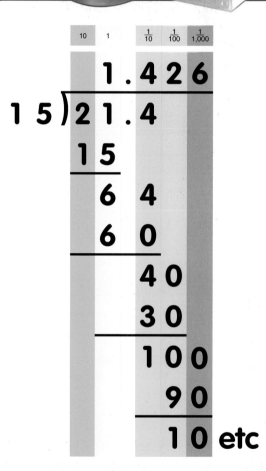

The answer was **1.426 centimetres**. Then he repeated the experiment with his CD boxes. You might like to try this with your boxes.

 Remember... To divide whole numbers into decimals, you can use either short or long division.

Can you do this?
12.6 ÷ 12 = ?

Work the answer out on a separate piece of paper.

Fractions to decimals

Decimals and fractions are two ways of showing the same thing. Here is how to convert between them.

This scale is decimal; **0.1**, **0.2** etc.

You need only to divide the top number (**numerator**) of a fraction by the bottom number (**denominator**) to get a decimal.

Numerator

$$\frac{3}{4}$$

Denominator

By short division, ³⁄₄ works out to **0.75** exactly.

| 1 | $\frac{1}{10}$ | $\frac{1}{100}$ | $\frac{1}{1,000}$ | $\frac{1}{10,000}$ |

$$4\overline{)3.0^{3}0^{2}00}$$
$$0.7500$$

You can ignore these zeros

If the numbers are easy, you might be able to do that in your head, and you will soon remember the common ones. For example ³⁄₄ (three-quarters) is exactly **0.75**.

$$\frac{3}{4} = 0.75$$

Here is another example – we will look at the fraction ⁹⁄₄.

$$\frac{9}{4}$$

By short division, ⁹⁄₄ works out to **2.25** exactly. We worked it out like this...

$$4\overline{)9.0^{1}0^{2}00}$$
$$2.2500$$

This scale is divided into fractional lengths of ½, ¼, etc.

It's common to see fractions and decimals together, as on this ruler.

Common conversions

Here are some more conversions that are often used in everyday life. Try to remember these.

$\frac{1}{10}$ (one tenth) = 0.1

$\frac{1}{100}$ (one hundredth) = 0.01

$\frac{1}{1000}$ (one thousandth) = 0.001

$\frac{1}{2}$ (one half) = 0.5

$\frac{1}{4}$ (one quarter) = 0.25

$\frac{3}{4}$ (three-quarters) = 0.75

$\frac{1}{5}$ (one fifth) = 0.2

$\frac{1}{8}$ (one eighth) = 0.125

$\frac{3}{8}$ (three-eighths) = 0.375

$\frac{5}{8}$ (five-eighths) = 0.625

$\frac{7}{8}$ (seven-eighths) = 0.875

Can you do this?

On a piece of paper write the fraction $\frac{22}{7}$ as a decimal. Stop after three decimal places.

 Remember... Every fraction can be converted into a decimal by dividing the top number by the bottom number.

Recurring decimals

A recurring decimal is one which never ends. This is what to do about such decimals.

One-third (⅓) is a very common fraction. It converts into a recurring decimal. Here is the working, done by long division.

3 divides into **10**, **3** times with a remainder of **1**. Bring down a **0**... and **3** divides into **10**, **3** times with a remainder of **1**... And so on, for ever.

The answer is: **0.3333333333333333 3333333333333333333333333...** for ever. Mathematicians say this as 'point three recurring'.

$$
\begin{array}{r}
0.3\ 3\ 3\ 3\ 3 \\
3\overline{)1.0\ 0\ 0\ 0\ 0} \\
9 \\
\hline
1\ 0 \\
9 \\
\hline
1\ 0 \\
9 \\
\hline
1\ 0 \\
9 \\
\hline
1\ 0 \\
9 \\
\hline
\textbf{etc}
\end{array}
$$

Not exactly...

Of course, **0.33** (using just the first two decimal places) is not exactly one-third.

The decimal number **0.33** is exactly the same as the fraction ³³/₁₀₀, and that is a little less than a third (⅓), as you can see by multiplying it by **3**. So, **3 × 33 = 99**.

The total is ⁹⁹/₁₀₀, which is a little less than **1**.

0.333 is not exactly one-third either.

The decimal number **0.333** is precisely the same as the fraction ³³³/₁₀₀₀, and that is also a little less than a third (⅓), as you can see by multiplying it by **3**. So, **3 × 333 = 999**.

The total is ⁹⁹⁹/₁₀₀₀, which is a little less than **1**.

That can go on infinitely too. But if the decimal **0.33333333333333333333333333** goes on for ever, it will be exactly one third.

$$3 \times 0.33 = \frac{99}{100}$$

$$3 \times 0.333 = \frac{999}{1000}$$

Here is a story to help you see why that should be the case:

Eating ice cream for ever and ever…

Gill has a **1 kg** (or **1,000 g**) tub of ice cream to share between **9** children. They are very eager to see that it is shared equally.

She cannot measure exactly ¹⁄₉ th of a kilogram, so she measures ¹⁄₁₀ th (**0.1 kg**, or **100 g**). The children each have a ¹⁄₁₀ th portion, and instead of eating the tenth portion herself, Gill keeps it for 'second helpings'.

Since this portion is **100 g**, she divides it in the same way, keeping one portion back for 'third helpings' and giving each child **10 g** or **0.01 kg**.

Using this system, the children could go on eating smaller and smaller portions of ice cream for ever!

If Gill could go on dividing it in the same way until there was absolutely none left, each child would have had exactly ¹⁄₉ th of it.

This tells us the very strange result that:

0.1 + 0.01 + 0.001 + 0.0001 + and so on for ever…

$$= \frac{1}{9} \text{ exactly.}$$

≫≫ **Remember…** A recurring decimal never ends.

Can you do this? On a piece of paper write down ⁴⁄₉ as a recurring decimal. When you have written down a lot of figures, add dots…

Rounding decimals

Calculators give a 'stampede' of numbers after the decimal point. So how do you cope with the answer?

Calculators do not have a brain to tell them what degree of accuracy to work towards. For example, when you divide **639** by **56** (639 ÷ 56) using a calculator, you get **11.41071429**.

It is best to keep working with these long numbers until you reach the very end of your calculation. They help your calculator give you the most accurate answer.

But, as you probably only need a short final answer, perhaps with only a tenths digit and a hundredths digit, you have to 'chop off' the string of numbers the calculator produces. This is called rounding off.

Use your calculator...
1. Enter **639**
2. Press division sign (/ or ÷)
3. Enter **56**
4. Press equals sign (=)
(Answer reads **11.41071429**)

Rounding up or down

Once you know what degree of accuracy you need, include one extra digit, and throw the rest away. In this example we have a figure showing **7.1421342** on our calculator, and we want only two decimal places (that is, to include tenths and hundredths).

The rule is this: if the extra digit is **0**, **1**, **2**, **3** or **4**, throw that away, too. But if it is **5**, **6**, **7**, **8**, **9**, then increase the last digit of the number we intend to keep by **1**, and then throw the final digit away.

Below are the numbers you throw away.

1	$\frac{1}{10}$	$\frac{1}{100}$

7.1 4 2 1̶3̶4̶2̶

7.1 4 2

If you want an answer that is accurate to **2** decimal places, look at the third decimal place. Since it is less than **5**, we can throw it and all of the extra numbers away.

32

Take a look at another example:

$$\frac{6}{7} = 0.8571428$$

We want an answer that is correct to **2** decimal places, so we throw away the fourth decimal and beyond.

Throw these away.

0.857~~1428~~

This is the extra digit that you do not need for a **2**-decimal-place answer.

But we see that the third decimal is **7**.

0.857

Since the final number is **7**, increase the last digit of the numbers we intend to keep by **1**, making the **5** into a **6**.

0.867

So we change the last digit in our answer to **6**.

0.86

Now we throw the **7** away.

This diagram shows why we increased the last digit. Clearly, **0.857** is closer to **0.86** than it is to **0.85**, which is why it is rounded up to **0.86**.

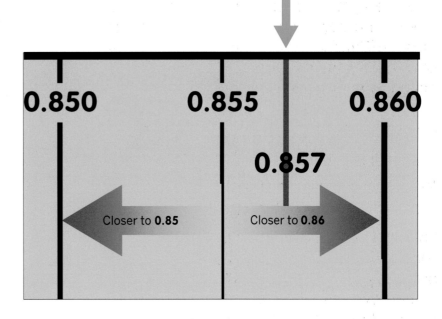

| 0.850 | 0.855 | 0.860 |

0.857

Closer to **0.85**   Closer to **0.86**

Can you do these in your head?
Round off these answers to two places of decimals.

721 ÷ 11 = 65.545455
1,066 ÷ 721 = 1.4785021

Write the answers on a separate piece of paper.

Remember... Decimal numbers are often rounded off. But remember to check the size of the digit just after the last one you want to keep to see if you need to round up or down.

Decimals to fractions

Turning decimals into fractions is not always so easy. Here are some hints.

Decimals with an end in sight

These are the simpler ones. To convert a decimal into a fraction, start by multiplying the decimal by **10**, **100**, or whatever number is needed to make the decimal into a whole number. Then simplify the fraction. For example:

0.4 can be made into a whole number if multiplied by **10**.

The calculation is:

$$0.4 = \frac{4}{10} \text{ (four-tenths)}$$

Now simplify the fraction by dividing the top and bottom numbers by **2**.

$$= \frac{2}{5} \text{ (two-fifths)}$$

$4 \div 2$

$10 \div 2$

Other multiples of tenths are just as easy:

$$0.3 = \frac{3}{10} \text{ (three-tenths)}$$

$$0.07 = \frac{7}{100} \text{ (seven-hundredths)}$$

$$0.25 = \frac{25}{100} \text{ (twenty-five-hundredths)}$$

$$= \frac{1}{4} \text{ (one-quarter)}$$

$25 \div 25$

$100 \div 25$

Pi, the impossible one!

There are some decimals which never end and never recur. However many decimal places are worked out, no repeating pattern can ever be found. There are lots of numbers like this, and a few of them are important.

The most famous is Pi. This is the number that you have to multiply the diameter of a circle by to find the circumference.

Throughout history mathematicians have devoted many years to calculating Pi to hundreds of decimal places. This was not because they needed to draw very accurate circles, but because they wanted to express Pi as an exact fraction, and so they hoped that the decimal would eventually recur.

In 1882 it was proved that it never, ever would. So people now accept using a close approximate fraction of ²²/₇.

3.141592653...

...is approximately equal to $\frac{22}{7}$

Pi to 1,000 decimal places is:

3.1415926535897932384626433832795028841971693993751058209749445923078164062862089986280348253421170679821480865132823066470938446095505822317253594081284811174502841027019385211055596446229489549303819644288109756659334461284756482337867831652712019091456485669234603486104543266482133936072602491412737245870066063155881748815209209628292540917153643678925903600113305305488204665213841469519415116094330572703657595919530921861173819326117931051185480744623799627495673518857527248912279381830119491298336733624406566430860213949463952247371907021798609437027705392171762931767523846748184676694051320005681271452635608277857713427577896091736371787214684409012249534301465495853710507922796892589235420199561121290219608640344181598136297747713099605187072113499999983729780499510597317328160963185950244594553469083026425223082533446850352619311881710100031378387528865875332083814206171776691473035982534904287554687311595628638823537875937519577818577805321712268066130019278766111959092164201989

Dividing decimals

To divide by a decimal make the number you are dividing by into a whole number first.

Enough for all?

Kyle's class was doing a science experiment by boiling salty water to find its temperature. His teacher mixed up **1.5 litres** of salty water.

Brian was given a scoop holding **85 millilitres** to make up to a **1 litre** solution of salty water.

Claudia had to use two scoops of salty water before doing the same, Toto had to use three scoops, Elizabeth had to use four scoops, and Kyle had to use five scoops.

Kyle was worried that there would not be enough salty water left when it was his turn. He worked out that at least **15** scoops would be needed. He added up his friends scoops like this: **1 + 2 + 3 + 4 + 5 = 15**. To work out whether there will be enough salty water left, he needed to divide **1.5 litres** by **85 millilitres**. Since there are **1,000 millilitres** in a litre, Kyle worked out that **85 millilitres** was equal to **0.085 litres**.

85 millilitres = 0.085 litre

The problem that Kyle needed to solve, was therefore **1.5** divided by **0.085**.

1.5 ÷ 0.085 = ?

Multiplying to remove the decimal point

One way around this difficult-looking problem is to turn the decimals into whole numbers by multiplying everything by **1,000**. In this way **0.085** becomes **85** and **1.5** becomes **1,500**. The division itself hasn't changed because all the numbers were multiplied by the same amount to express them as millilitres.

Now we can use long division. The answer is that there would be **17.6** scoops available.

Clearly this is more than the **15** needed. Kyle need not have worried that there would not be enough for him!

Also...

In Kyle's calculation the decimal point disappeared from the number he divided by (the divisor) as well as the number he divided into (the dividend). This does not always happen. The important thing is to remember to make the divisor into a whole number before you divide.

1,000	100	10	1	$\frac{1}{10}$

$$
\begin{array}{r}
17.6 \\
85\overline{)1500.0} \\
85 \\
\hline
650 \\
595 \\
\hline
550 \\
510 \\
\hline
40 \text{ etc}
\end{array}
$$

Remember... To divide decimal numbers easily, you need to multiply both divisor and dividend by the same number of **10's** until the divisor is a whole number.

Can you do these?

5.5 ÷ 0.25 (Imagine they are £, and convert them both to pence before dividing.)

7.5 ÷ 0.035 (Imagine they are litres, and convert them both to ml before dividing.)

Give your working out on a separate piece of paper.

Comparing decimals

Here's how to compare decimal numbers quickly and easily.

Everybody knows that **207** is bigger than **34**. We know this because **207** has a **2** in the hundreds column while **34** has nothing in the hundreds column. This is true even though **34** has three tens and **207** doesn't have any.

It works the same way with decimals. A decimal with something in the tenths column must be bigger than another decimal with **0** in the tenths column.

Units	Tenths of a unit	Hundredths of a unit

0 . 1 1 This number contains tenths

is bigger than

0 . 0 9 This number contains only hundredths, there are no tenths.

Comparing significant figures

If the digits in the first decimal place are different, the one with the bigger digit is the bigger number. So, for example **0.8239** is bigger than **0.74589** as shown on the right.

If the first digits are the same, we compare the second digits in the same way.

If the first and second digits are the same, the one with the bigger third digit is the bigger number.

And so on.

0 . 8 2 3 9
is bigger than
0 . 7 4 5 8 9
or **0.8239 > 0.74589**

0 . 5 6 8
is bigger than
0 . 5 5 9
or **0.568 > 0.559**

0 . 3 9 7
is bigger than
0 . 3 9 5
or **0.397 > 0.395**